Wisdom for Leaders

Boyd Bailey

Cover designed by Max Prince
© 2014 Wisdom Hunters, LLC
Published by Wisdom Hunters, LLC
http://www.wisdomhunters.com
Book ISBN: 978-0615967226

INTRODUCTION

My leadership ebbs and flows in effectiveness based on how well I follow Jesus. If I follow Jesus well, I tend to lead well. When I run ahead of the Lord, I leave those I am entrusted to lead too far behind. I am learning I can't lead from a distance. I must be relationally engaged up close. Like the nub of a melted, flickering candle, my influence wanes when in my exuberance, I am way out front. Thus, my goal is to daily walk with Christ, so I can prayerfully lead our team.

Leadership is hard, growing as a leader is harder, and growing leaders is hardest. It is hard, since it sometimes requires an unpopular decision that moves us and others out of our comfort zones. It's harder to grow as a leader, because it means we remain teachable, we listen well, and we make difficult character changes. We grow as we evaluate our experiences and apply lessons learned to our leadership. It's hardest to grow leaders, inasmuch as it requires our consistent investment in individuals with potential. Many disappoint, some show promise, and a very few flourish.

"Be strong in the grace that is in Christ Jesus. And the things that you have heard from me among many witnesses, commit these to faithful men who will be able to teach others also" (2 Timothy 2:1-2, NKJV).

How do you measure your leadership effectiveness? Perhaps you start by asking those you lead how well you are doing. Be vulnerable to their feedback related to your emotional intelligence of their skills and gifts. What motivates them? Private words of affirmation, quality time with you and the team, public recognition, gifts, or time off, are a few motivations that could move them to stellar performance. Leaders who listen well to their team, understand what motivates their team.

Moreover, we may not be the most charismatic or brilliant leader, but by God's grace we can all be wise leaders. Wisdom is a gift from the Lord that He imparts to those with a heart of integrity and humility. Our openness to receive wisdom from above allows us to lead effectively below, here on earth, as Christ's ambassador. After all, our ability to lead like Jesus means we must employ the mind of Christ. He is wisdom and by faith, He lives within our heart.

"Christ the power of God and the wisdom of God" (1 Corinthians 1:24, NKJV).

The leader who models the way, shows the way. If we wander away from our responsibilities, some team members will lose focus. The speed of the leader is the speed of the team. The interest of the leader is the interest of the team. The intensity of the leader is the intensity of the team. Like a rising tide lifts all boats, so the faith of the leader lifts the faith of all team members. A great work is sustained by great leaders who remain engaged in the execution of the mission. Therefore, lean into the Lord and learn from Him. Jesus is gentle and gracious to refresh you, so you in turn, can refresh the team. Your leadership depends on hearing from your heavenly Father.

"I do nothing on my own but speak just what the Father has taught me" (John 8:28).

OTHER BOOKS BY BOYD BAILEY

Seeking Daily the Heart of God, Volume I – a 365-day Devotional
Seeking Daily the Heart of God, Volume II – a 365-day Devotional
Infusion – a 90-day Devotional
Seeking God in the Psalms – a 90-day Devotional
Seeking God in the Proverbs – a 90-day Devotional
Wisdom for Graduates – a 30-day Devotional
Wisdom for Mothers – a 30-day Devotional
Wisdom for Fathers – a 30-day Devotional
Wisdom for Marriage – a 30-day Devotional
Wisdom for Work – a 30-day Devotional
Wisdom for Money – a 30-day Devotional

JOIN OUR ONLINE COMMUNITY

SIGN UP for your free "Wisdom Hunters...Right Thinking" daily
devotional e-mail at **wisdomhunters.com**
"LIKE" us on Facebook at **facebook.com/wisdomhunters**
FOLLOW us on Twitter at **twitter.com/wisdomhunters**
SUBSCRIBE to us on YouTube at
youtube.com/wisdomhuntersvids
DOWNLOAD the free Wisdom Hunters App for
tablets and mobile devices on iTunes and Google Play

TABLE OF CONTENTS

1

God Chosen

"Then the LORD said to Moses, 'See, I have chosen Bezalel son of Uri, the son of Hur, of the tribe of Judah, and I have filled him with the Spirit of God, with skill, ability and knowledge in all kinds of crafts...'"
Exodus 31:1-3

God uses whom He chooses, and He equips those He calls. When there is a vision to be cast, a mission to be accomplished, or a task to be completed, Christ's call is to specific people for a specific purpose. The call of Christ is humbling, but His call is real, nonetheless. It is a call to obedience, first and foremost. Will you say yes to Yahweh's call? He will grow you into the leader you need to be, but the Holy Spirit directs an obedient follower, not one stuck in the inertia of safety.

You can be sure that your faithfulness in managing His giftedness matters. God chooses those who have been faithful with what may at first seem like small gifts. Your Lord is not slack in anointing and equipping you for the task. There is no vision that overwhelms your Father in heaven. He fills with His Spirit those who surrender to Him. When you submit as His chosen one, His Spirit indwells and empowers you for His assignment.

Therefore, let the Lord drive your spiritual development. Stay submitted, surrendered, and obedient, and He will fill, anoint, and baptize you in His spirit. This is not some mystical maneuvering; it is God's way of emboldening your faith and consecrating your character. Watch in wonder as He hones your skills. His desire for your next season of service is that your knowledge and abilities be elevated to a whole new level.
This may mean more formal education, or informal mentoring from more experienced men and women. It may require self-education and on-the-job training. Or, it may require a combination of all these initiatives and more. Submit your parenting skills, your leadership skills, and your spiritual know-how to Him. Above all else, stay in Christ's school of prayer. The lessons learned in your prayer closet will instruct you way beyond what you can ask or think. "Now to him who is able to do immeasurably more than all we ask or imagine, according to his power that is at work within us" (Ephesians 3:20).

Prayer is an exchange of the natural with the supernatural. Prayer takes your finite understanding, and empowers it with eternity's infinite knowledge, wisdom, and discernment. Having the highest intelligence quotient is not what determines whether God chooses you. He chooses a heart that is hungry for His wisdom. It is a desire for wisdom that opens up the windows of heaven's resources. Prayer prepares your heart and mind to receive and apply the wisdom of God.

Equipping and training develops your skills and abilities for the assignment at hand, and experience will lift your leadership to a whole new level of total trust in the Lord. There are no insignificant assignments from the Almighty, so tackle your new role with abandon and passion. He has prepared you for this season, so don't look back. Just look forward to the Lord by faith. Be humbled. Be grateful. Be obedient. Be trusting. Do I trust Jesus that He has chosen me for my current role and responsibilities? "You did not choose me, but I chose you and appointed you to go and bear fruit—fruit that will last. Then the Father will give you whatever you ask in My name" (John 15:16).

Prayer: Heavenly Father lead me by Your Spirit to follow your calling on my life.

Related Readings: 1 Chronicles 28:6; Isaiah 43:10; Romans 16:13; 1 Peter 2:4

2

Focused Leadership

Brothers, I do not consider myself yet to have taken hold of it.
But one thing I do: Forgetting what is behind and
straining toward what is ahead.
Philippians 3:13

Paul understood and applied focused leadership. Under extreme conditions he remained vigilant to plant churches and preach the gospel, even in the face of hostile resistance. So, in uncertain times, I have to look into the mirror and ask, 'Am I focused on the task at hand, or am I distracted by critics and circumstances?' Focused leadership finds a way.

Perhaps you take a more direct leadership role, so the team can draft off your intensity. For example, consider attending or even leading the sales meetings for a season. Help the team discover creative ways to retain current customers and attract new ones. Be available to serve in ways and at times that strategically create momentum and excel execution. Focused leadership strips back to the essentials of getting the right results.

Focused leadership also applies at home. If finances have spiraled out of control, the husband is to take responsibility and lovingly lead his wife and children to wise and frugal expenditures. Everyone sacrifices something during tight economic times. You may need to sell a car, or explain to your teenager the only affordable option is in-state tuition.

Until you change, the organization or your family won't. Apathy and inertia are not options; the focused leader allows only intense interest and forward motion. Draw a circle around your feet, kneel down and ask God for wisdom and discernment, starting with your own leadership transformation. Focus on your Heavenly Father and He will lead you to successfully lead. Prayerfully ask, 'Is my heart on Him?' "I consider everything a loss compared to the surpassing greatness of knowing Christ Jesus my Lord..." (Philippians 3:8a).

Prayer: Heavenly Father keep me focused to follow Your heart and plan.

Related Readings: Joshua 1:7; 1 Kings 8:61; Luke 10:42; 1 Corinthians 9:24-27

3

Gift of Leadership

If it is to encourage, then give encouragement; if it is giving,
then give generously; if it is to lead, do it diligently;
if it is to show mercy, do it cheerfully.
Romans 12:8

Gifted leaders are first and foremost good followers of God. They recognize the Gift Giver as their authority, so they do not lord over others—rather they submit themselves to the Lord. Because the leader respects Christ, he or she respects those they lead. Because they love the Lord, they love their team. Because they serve Jesus, they serve those who serve with them. Yes, a gifted leader is able to influence and educate a group toward an agreed upon goal. Leaders have followers.

Are you called to lead but feel inferior? If so, seek your confidence in Christ. Go to the Resourceful One for reassurance. Resistance does not mean you are a bad leader; on the contrary it may be a validation that you are moving in the right direction. Indeed, some struggle with getting on the bandwagon of change—it threatens their security. So stay the course and lead prayerfully, patiently and lovingly. Trust the Spirit's small voice that affirms your actions—God is with you.

"Love must be sincere. Hate what is evil; cling to what is good. Be devoted to one another in love. Honor one another above yourselves. Never be lacking in zeal, but keep your spiritual fervor, serving the Lord. Be joyful in hope, patient in affliction, faithful in prayer." Romans 12:9-12

You know you have the gift of leadership if you can see the big picture and inspire others toward that God-given vision. You understand the sequence of steps required to reach the objectives. You perceive potential problems and are courageous and wise in making adjustments. You motivate the team to embrace transitions as necessary to stay relevant. You create a culture of accountability with real-time updates. No one wants to let anyone down in the execution process.

Your gift of leadership is a weighty responsibility, but you are not alone. Almighty God is your "go to" for humility, holiness and wisdom. God gives you what you need to accomplish what He wants. Furthermore, use your leadership role to invest in other emerging leaders. It is harder to grow leaders than it is to lead. Therefore, be intentional and prayerful to train up faithful men and women who will train others. You steward your leadership best by birthing other leaders!

"And David shepherded them with integrity of heart; with skillful hands he led them." Psalm 78:72

Prayer: Heavenly Father, lead me, so that in humility I can lead others in Your ways.

Related Readings: Exodus 32:21; 1 Samuel 18:16; Isaiah 48:21; 1 Timothy 6:11-12; 1 Corinthians 1:10

4

Character and Competence

Walk before Me, as David your father walked, in integrity of heart and uprightness, doing according to all that I have commanded you. keeping My statutes and My precepts.
1 Kings 9:4

Authentic leadership is a mixture of character and competence. You cannot have one without the other and provide healthy leadership. Competence without character is like a ship's magnificent ivory sail that lies collapsed without wind. Character without competence is like a strong gust of wind without a billowy sail to capture its effect. Both are required for the level of leadership that God expects. Character is the linchpin of leadership. It is truly the measure of a man.

Your character is your union card, it earns you the right to participate in leadership. Your depth of character determines your breadth of leadership. Character is forged on the anvil of life's experience. When your obedience to God intersects with life, character is developed. It is through a relationship with Christ and a relationship with people that you understand and develop character. God's Word defines character, and living life is your opportunity to apply character. You can choose to be a character, or you can seek to live a life of character.

God's will is the latter. People want leaders that are dependable. Someone they can trust. They want leaders that are available to listen and understand. A leader of character follows through on commitments and does what is right even when it costs him personally. You can have average skill with exceptional character and still be an extraordinary leader. This is how God works. He works from the inside out. Sometimes your great abilities get in the way of a definitive work of character in your life. Anything you have is because of the grace of God, so thank Him for your abilities and allow Him to mold His character into your life.

Competence on the other hand gives you a platform to exercise your character. You are gifted and skilled in certain ways. It is imperative that you understand how you are wired. This self-awareness is your ticket to improvement. What you know today is not sufficient for what you need to know tomorrow. This is why competent leaders are ever learning. Current circumstances and future opportunities beg for your education. Skilled leaders ask lots of questions of those who have walked before them. They research and read about other successful leadership and organizational models. This is part of sharpening your skills. When was the last time you took an eternal audit and valued your character?

What is the worth of your honesty, your hard work, your love, your servant leadership, your accountability, your generosity and your faith? Just as exercise and diet contribute to a healthy body, so character contributes to the health of your soul and emotions. "May God Himself, the God of peace, sanctify you through and through. May your whole spirit, soul and body be kept blameless at the coming of our Lord Jesus Christ" (1 Thessalonians 5:23).

Because character is like precious jewels, wisdom keeps it secure in the lock-box of your life. Assign faith and obedience as two sentinels poised at the entrance of your heart and mind. These loyal friends keep Satan from snatching away even a portion of your hard earned character. Indeed your investment in integrity is worth aggressive protection.

In your business, home or ministry it is of extreme worth to define the values that hold accountable everyone involved. Values are to a company what character is to an individual. What is the character you expect in the workplace and at home? Respect, excellence, thoroughness, trustworthiness, balance and faith-based may all be behaviors that reflect the character of your life at work, home and church. Seriously consider collaboration with all invested parties and define the desired character of the enterprise.

A stagnant leader is an unattractive leader. Focus on your sweet spot. Spend your time on the number one thing you do best. If it is recruiting, then recruit. If it is raising money, then raise money. If it is coaching, then coach. If it is crunching numbers, then crunch numbers. If it is managing a home, then manage a home. But, in the process, become the best at what you do and who you are. Yesterday's competency will not stand against today's needs.

Passion does not equal expertise. Just because you want to do something does not mean you need to do it. Make sure that your skill set and experience matches your "want to." Otherwise, you are setting yourself and others up for frustration. My passion will not improve my golf game unless I am skilled with hand-and-eye coordination. You can be sincere in your endeavors and still be involved in the wrong situation. Make sure you live and lead in environments that nurture and grow your giftedness.

This type of leadership development molds you into a leader worth following. Your competence gives you credibility, while your character sustains your credibility. Apply both, and then watch God work. Character with competence is your ticket to authentic leadership. Let these two be your guide, and God will use you beyond your own capabilities. Lead on!

Prayer: Heavenly Father I pray my character keeps up with the success of my competence.

Related Readings: Genesis 5:24; 6:9; Romans 6:11; 1 Corinthians 1:30

Daily Wisdom in Your Inbox... A Free Subscription: www.wisdomhunters.com

5

Pride's Presumption

Do not go up, because the Lord is not with you. You will be
defeated by your enemies... Nevertheless, in their presumption
they went up toward the high hill country, though neither
Moses nor the ark of the Lord's covenant moved from the camp...
[Their enemies] who lived in that hill country came down and
attacked them and beat them down.
Numbers 14:42, 44-45b

Pride presumes. It presumes on people and, more disturbingly, it presumes on God. It manipulates on behalf of "my" agenda. When you and I presume, we take matters into our own hands. Presumption is a big price to pay for forced results. You think you can do just about anything if you have enough time, money and will power.

But, is this really the will of God? Should you even do this, or are your motives a product of your pride—presuming that the good times will keep on rolling? Everything you touched in the past may have turned to gold, but past success cannot justify future presumption. Instead, stay sharp and dependent on God.

When you first started out, there was a respect and a dependence on God that defined you daily. Don't lose this. When you slip from dependence on God to presuming on God, you are set up for failure. God will not be used. This is not His style nor the style of discerning leaders. Indeed, before you charge ahead, make sure others are up to speed and on board with your goals and His plan.

You may artificially bend another's will, but eventually your subtle presumption of their loyalty will break their spirit and drive them away. They will not be taken for granted. It is a matter of respect. Will we respect the wishes of others, or will we plow ahead with a wake of relational wreckage behind us? Certain assumptions need to be questioned.

The team that served you with excellence up until now may not be the team that takes you to the next level. Or, you may be the one who needs to be replaced. Do not presume that your level of leadership skills has the capacity to carry on the expansion of the enterprise. Presumption is painful and painstaking. Avoid it at all costs.

Presumption on God is the most serious derivative of pride. Religious pride subtly uses God to manipulate people and circumstances. It is sad but true. If left unchecked, God gets saddled with our immature goals and desires. Sometimes the desired outcome is noble, but the timing is unwise. A building program is a worthy goal, but it becomes presumptive if the last facility is unpaid for and the future one needs to be highly leveraged by debt.

Don't drag God into poor planning and ask Him to bless it after the fact. Scripture is the Word of God. However, if a Bible verse is ripped from its context to prove a point of presumption, then it becomes a facilitator of deception. Do not use the Holy Bible for worldly outcomes. You cannot presume that the Scripture supports your desires just because it seems right. Emotion can lead you down the dead-end road of presumption.

Therefore, keep pride's presumption in check with humility's trust. Humility trusts God to come through without having to mandate or manipulate. Humility patiently waits on people. You can have a sense of eternal urgency without being disrespectful or demanding. Pride, without fear of God as a check and balance, will drive you ahead in your presumption. Humility first seeks out the Lord in a quiet spot and listens for His voice of validation.

Pride will push you to presume. Humility will invite you to trust. Trust God's promises, but do not presume that He will bless your pride. Pride's presumption will lead to your downfall. Humility's trust will lead to your success. Therefore, take a step back, wait, pray, listen and make sure the Lord is with you!

Prayer: Heavenly Father keep my heart humble and dependent on You.

Related Readings: Proverbs 16:18-20; Psalm 10:4; Proverbs 22:4

6

Leadership in Adversity

After that, he poured water into a basin and began to wash his
disciples' feet, drying them with the towel that was
wrapped around him.
John 13:5

Adversity invites leaders to lead. It is your time to trust the Lord and lead by faith, not fear. In hard times a leader asks, "Will I panic or pray?" "Will I stay calm or be sucked into the chaos?" "Will I serve the team or stay secluded in silence?" Jesus faced death, but He was determined to stay focused on His heavenly Father and the mission at hand. Adversity is an opportunity to prove the point of Providence. Christ is in control.

How can you use adversity to your advantage as a leader? One way is to unify the team around common objectives and goals. There is no better way to bring people together than in the fires of hardship and difficulty. In fact, you probably will not succeed without the team rising to its next level of leadership and team support. So reward creativity, because limitations lead to innovation. Lead the team to accomplish more with less.

Paul said, "We put no stumbling block in anyone's path, so that our ministry will not be discredited. Rather, as servants of God we commend ourselves in every way: in great endurance; in troubles, hardships and distresses" (2 Corinthians 6:3–4).

Moreover, use hard times to create a culture of hard work and honesty. It may mean longer hours and less pay, but sacrifice is the price to be paid for productivity. Invite honest feedback so you accurately and effectively improve process and products. Raise team expectations beyond just surviving to thriving. They look to you for leadership; so lead.

Lastly, serve at home and work with appreciation. It is easy to demand more and more while under pressure and forget to say "Thank you." Perhaps you give the team a day off, leave a grateful voicemail, buy everyone lunch, or send flowers. Wise leaders honestly inquire, "How can I outserve others, especially in the face of misfortune?" "Where do I need to take responsibility, not blaming outside forces?" Leaders model the way.

Jesus said, "I have set you an example that you should do as I have done for you" (John 13:15).

How can I out serve others, especially in the face of misfortune? Where do I need to take responsibility, not blaming outside forces?

Related Readings: Exodus 4:28–30; 1 Samuel 17:22–24; Acts 10:4–8

7

Leaders Have Followers

Follow me and I will make you fishers of men...
Matthew 4:19

People followed Jesus. This was a key indicator of His leadership, because leaders have followers. Small groups sought Him out for discipleship. The masses mobbed Him for His miracles and authoritative teaching, and individuals clamored for His hope and healing. So I have to ask myself, "When I look behind me are people following?"

People follow those they respect; whom they regard as a trustworthy person of character, and a person of competence who executes strategy with excellence. However, as with Jesus, followers can become fatigued and fall away during times of trials. Leaders are sometimes left alone to bear their cross, die on the cross and be resurrected to the renewal of a vast vision. Leaders like Jesus will experience unpleasant days. But, it is during these days of dire straits that the Spirit gives us strength.

"That is why, for Christ's sake, I delight in weaknesses, in insults, in hardships, in persecutions, in difficulties. For when I am weak, then I am strong". 2 Corinthians 12:10

Furthermore, Jesus was a tough leader on occasion. He said hard things during hard times. For example, He told an insubordinate Peter, "Get behind me Satan" (Matthew 16:23). This was a test of his motivation and faith. It is during these defining moments that you either lose a good person, or gain a great one. Moreover, Jesus' style of leadership was loving and patient. He was not in a hurry to heal the hurt of Mary and Martha's grief, but when He ultimately arrived, He cared deeply (John 11:32-33). Leadership is about being in the right place at the right time for the right reasons.

Therefore, do not react hastily in fear, but respond patiently in faith. Your family is your laboratory for leadership, so serve them well and serve them often. Look around you at work and seek to understand the needs of your team—take the time to look behind and ask, "Is anyone following me?" Above all, be a faithful follower of Jesus, no matter what.

"Then he [Jesus] got into the boat and his disciples followed him". Matthew 8:23

When I look behind me, can I honestly say others are enthusiastically following my leadership; if not, why?

Related Readings: Exodus 18:25; Numbers 27:18; John 12:42; Hebrews 13:7

8

Too Familiar Leaders

Obey your leaders and submit to their authority. They keep watch over you as men who must give an account. Obey them so that their work will be a joy, not a burden, for that would be of no advantage to you.
Hebrews 13:17

Leaders can become so familiar with their team that they dilute their effectiveness to lead. They are not one of the boys or one of the girls—they are the leader. Parents have to learn this. They are not the child or teenager's friend—they are first the dad or mom. Friendship can come later with adult children; in the meantime, they need leadership.

So how familiar are you with those you lead? Are you respectful of others so you invite their respect? Do you lift them up with commendation or tear them down with coarse kidding? Joking around on the job is not a pattern great leaders model. This may have been your behavior in the past, but in the present your role requires more maturity.

Does this mean leaders are not transparent about their weaknesses? No, because humble leaders are the first to confess their struggles and blind spots. But it does mean that wise leaders approach their God-given role with solemn responsibility and serious resolve. People need leaders they can trust and look up to as the Lord's leaders for this season.

We do not want those we lead to pray as David did: "May his days be few; may another take his place of leadership" (Psalm 109:8). Followers want to be led by a wise leader.

Moreover, when we become too close to a team member, it creates jealousy, rivalry, and resentment. This happens with children. If we play favorites with a child, other siblings will notice and spew out their frustrations on the parent's pet. We can reward good behavior and praise obedience, but we should not overdo it by crossing the line of becoming too familiar.

Leadership can be lonely, but we are not alone as followers of Jesus. Wise leaders keep their emotions under the Spirit's control in the presence of their team, but in the presence of the Lord they bare their soul. You cannot become too familiar with your heavenly Father. He already knows more about you than you do. Pour out your frustrations and fears to Him, and He will listen, forgive, and lead you in the way you should go.

"My tears have been my food day and night, while men say to me all day long, 'Where is your God?' These things I remember as I pour out my soul: how I used to go with the multitude, leading the procession to the house of God, with shouts of joy and thanksgiving among the festive throng. Why are you downcast, O my soul? Why so disturbed within me? Put your hope in God, for I will yet praise him, my Savior and my God" (Psalm 42:3–5).

Prayer: Do I look to the Lord to lead me? How can I lovingly lead with honesty and respect?

Related Readings: Exodus 18:13–16; Zechariah 12:5–6; John 12:42; Hebrews 13:7

9

Sober Leadership

It is not for kings, O Lemuel not for kings to drink wine, not for rulers to crave beer, lest they drink and forget what the law decrees, and deprive all the oppressed of their rights.
Proverbs 31:4-5

Sober leadership is needed for serious leaders, men and women who seek what's best for the team without being tempted by temporary inebriation. Alcohol and drugs can cause people in power to pretend one thing and do another. It is during casual circumstances that a leader can find their integrity compromised by participating in a too familiar behavior.

Leaders in the church are described in this way, "Deacons, likewise, are to be men worthy of respect, sincere, not indulging in much wine, and not pursuing dishonest gain. They must keep hold of the deep truths of the faith with a clear conscience." (1Timothy 3:8-9). Sober leadership sets the tone for other team members to follow their example. What the leader tolerates in moderation can be taken to the extreme by the less mature.

What are your guidelines to protect your decision-making? What behavior do you predetermine before attending a company party or a business trip where your associates expect shady social activities? It is easy to get sucked into a regrettable situation if there are no behavioral boundaries. Perhaps you stay focused on work during the work week and enjoy rest and relaxation with friends and family on the weekend. Mixing business and pleasure can prove to be an unproductive and destructive combination.

Sober leadership sends a message of sincerity and a sense of urgency. It is not void of joy and laughter, but there is an undertone of discipline and seriousness which invites loyalty. Stay sober as a leader and you will reap the rewards of respect and results. Ask others to confront your questionable decisions and actions. Fools flail away in confused thinking while sober minded leaders are clear-headed and humbled by God.

"Do not think of yourself more highly than you ought, but rather think of yourself with sober judgment..." (Romans 12:3b).

Is my leadership sober minded? Am I conscious of Christ's wisdom?

Related Readings: Exodus 18:25; 1 Samuel 25:26-28; Hebrews 13:7; 1 Timothy 3:1-7

10

Attitude Adjustment

For seven days they celebrated with joy the Feast of Unleavened Bread, because the Lord had filled them with joy by changing the attitude of the king of Assyria, so that he assisted them in the work on the house of God, the God of Israel.
Ezra 6:22

Attitude is everything; it can lift you up or bring you down. It is the barometer of your heart. If your heart is not right, your attitude will suffer. Attitude is critical because it influences your course of action. If your attitude is negative, then your words and your behavior will be too. There is a difference in being a realist about negative circumstances, and living with a chronic bad attitude. Naïve are those who ignore warning signs of trouble, and carry on oblivious to the storm clouds of sin. However, your attitude is rooted in who you are in Christ, so there is no need to be fearful, guilty, or insecure.

The attitude that Jesus exhibited was one of humility and servant leadership. His attitude reflected submission to His heavenly Father, which resulted in service, generosity, and love for people. Jesus was joyful and hopeful because He rested in the will of God. Do not allow others' bad attitude to influence yours. Be the attitude influencer instead. Greet a frown with a smile, crush criticism with affirmation, and listen patiently until fury loses its steam. A positive attitude will eventually outlast and overpower a negative one. Most of all, pray for those who thrive on negativity. Pray for them to be set free from their hurt, anger, guilt, and insecurity. God has you in their lives to reflect the Almighty and to encourage an attitude adjustment through Him.

God is the genesis of a right attitude. He is the right attitude sustainer. He wants His attitude to be our attitude. This is why you need a daily attitude alignment from your heavenly Father. Each day, your attitude gets knocked around and abused by life. If left unattended, your attitude will drift into wrong thinking, harsh words, and bad behavior. Self-pity and anger can begin to replace selflessness and forgiveness. With just a little bit of daily tweaking, your attitude stays in line with His. It is subtle, but sometimes attitudes need to be adjusted moment by moment.

Lastly, slow down and pray when you feel your attitude eroding. When you're in the midst of a bad attitude, don't make important decisions; the time isn't right for that. You will regret every decision you make during a time of emotional upheaval. Be patient, and wait until your anger has subsided, your heart is cleansed, and your attitude is objective. Almighty God is into attitudes that trust Him and reach out to others with compassion and understanding. Open-minded and reasonable attitudes lead to rich and robust relationships. Anyone can be negative; so don't be anyone, be different. Allow God to shape your attitude on the anvil of His heart.

An attitude molded by God is infectious and transforming. Allow Him to change yours, and then trust Him to change another's. The Bible says, "Your attitude should be the same as that of Christ Jesus..." (Philippians 2:5).

Prayer: Dear Lord give me an attitude of gratitude in my life and work.

Related Readings: Ezra 6:22; Ephesians 4:22-24: Romans 15:5

11

Follow Jesus First

When Jesus saw the crowd around him, he gave orders to cross to
the other side of the lake. Then a teacher of the law came to him
and said, "Teacher, I will follow you wherever you go."
Matthew 8:18-19

Good leaders are first good followers. Do you follow the orders of Jesus? When He asks you to do the uncomfortable, do you move out of your comfort zone with confidence? Compelling Christian leadership has focused followship on their Master, the Lord Jesus. Where is He asking you to go that requires sacrifice and unconditional commitment? His orders do not always make sense, but they are totally trustworthy and helpful.

When He directs you to leave the noise of the crowds to the quiet of a few, do not delay. If you are obsessed by activity, you can easily lose your edge on energy and faith. When all my oomph is consumed on serving every request and answering every call, I have no time or concentration to hear from Christ. What is He saying? This is the most important inquiry I can make. What is Jesus telling me to do? So, when I listen, I learn.

You may be in the middle of a monster season of success, so make sure your achievements do not muffle the Lord's message. It's when we are fast and furious that our faith becomes perfunctory and predictable. Leadership requires alone time to retool and recalibrate our character. People follow when they know you've been with Jesus.

The most difficult part may be the transition from doing less, to listening and thinking more. If you, as the leader, are not planning ahead, who is? Who has the best interest of the enterprise in mind? Who is defending the mission and vision of the organization, so there is not a drift into competing strategies? Follow Jesus first, then He frees you to see.

Where is the Lord leading you to go? Will you lag behind with excellent excuses, or will you make haste and move forward by faith? Go with God and He will direct you through the storms of change. He may seem silent at times, but remember He led you to this place, and where He leads, He provides. Follow Jesus first, and go wherever He goes. You will lose people in the process, but you will gain better people for His next phase.

"Then Jesus said to his disciples, "If anyone would come after me, he must deny himself and take up his cross and follow me" (Matthew 6:24).

Where is Jesus leading me to go? Am I willing to let go and trust Him with what's next?

Related Readings: Numbers 32:11; Isaiah 8:10-12; 1 Corinthians 1:11-13; Revelation 14:4

12

Giant Opportunities

"The LORD said to Moses, 'Send some men to explore the land
of Canaan, which I am giving to the Israelites...' Then Caleb silenced
the people before Moses and said, 'We should go up and take
possession of the land, for we can certainly do it.' But the men who
had gone up with him said, 'We can't attack those people;
they are stronger than we are.'"
Numbers 13:1a, 30-31

As we face life, we can be overwhelmed by its giant obstacles or be inspired by its giant opportunities. Challenges and uncertainties tend to corrode our confidence. It is in the face of the unknown that we can move forward by faith, or backward in disbelief. What giant obstacles are you facing? How can your obstacles be converted into opportunities? Obstacles are stepping stones for obedient feet to follow.

Therefore, stay focused with aggressive patience and you will eventually see some obstacles dissolve while others are transformed into treasures. Possibly a financial opportunity is looming large but it seems like an intimidating obstacle. If so, stay true to your integrity by not selectively suspending your core values for much needed results. Instead, remain faithful to wise stewardship and honesty. The right results will follow at the right time. Trust God to use scary giants for His glory.

God orchestrates giant opportunities for His greater good. He told Moses that He was giving His children the promised land; all they had to do was show up and receive His gift. Giant opportunities often require faith, planning, perseverance, and hard work, but sometimes the reward of obedience and trust in the Lord is enough. So how are you facing the giants in your life; as obstacles or opportunities?

Leaders look and pray for opportunities, exploring them with energy and enthusiasm. Your relentless leadership inspires your family, friends, and work associates to remain faithful and not freak out. Therefore, take the opportunity the Lord has given you. Difficult days and economic challenges are great opportunities for God to get the glory. So be aggressive, increase your efforts, actively pursue heaven with prayer, and by faith receive what your Savior Jesus has already given you. Go after the giant opportunities with gusto and with grace.

The Bible says, "I can do all things through Him who strengthens me" (Philippians 4:13, NASB).

Prayer: With what giant obstacle can I trust God to turn it into an opportunity?

Related Readings: Joshua 14:6-8; Isaiah 41:10-16; Romans 8:31-37; Hebrews 11:33

13

Just Say No

Simply let your "Yes" be "Yes," and your "No," "No"; anything
beyond this comes from the evil one.
Matthew 5:37

Is it hard for you to say "no"? No to opportunities? No to temptation? No to a child? No to your spouse? No to good things? No to bad things? A a leader your no is probably more important than your yes. When you muster the courage to resist an idea that is off mission and instill the discipline in your team to stay focused on the task at hand, you lead with courage. The power of saying no makes your yes more believable.

How can a man or woman's leadership be effective if they say yes to everything? Is a spontaneous "yes" nearly as useful as a measured "no"? Instead of making a rash promise you later regret, why not wait and prayerfully think through the resources required to deliver on your commitment? Short-term appeasement dilutes long-term sustainability.

Yes, you do risk rejection when you say no, but over time the wisdom of your decision will become more evident. For example, resist taking on debt for a major purchase like a wedding, a car, a vacation or an appliance. Instead, save up your cash, and look for deals and creative alternatives in the meantime. Why saddle yourself with the stress of paying for something you can't afford now, so that you can peacefully enjoy it credit free in the future?

Moreover, you may not have peace about a particular career opportunity. There are too many unknowns and those who know you best are tentative. Perhaps you prayerfully say no now and trust the Lord to provide an open door that aligns with His will later. Do not decide out of frustration or in the middle of fatigue. Instead, rest, gather a clear head and see what your heart has to say. Default to "no" until you "know".

"Teach me your way, O LORD, and I will walk in your truth; give me an undivided heart, that I may fear your name" (Psalm 86:11).

As a leader at home and at work, be more focused on saying no than yes. Tough love often defines reality by saying no. But make sure to express your denial with grace. When you communicate bad news in the spirit of Jesus it can become good news to the recipient.

This is how His enemies described Him, ""Teacher, we know that you speak and teach what is right, and that you do not show partiality but teach the way of God in accordance with the truth" (Luke 20:11).

Do I have the courage to trust Christ and say no even when it is offensive? How can I learn to say no more often with patience and grace?

Related Readings: Proverbs 3:5-6; Proverbs 16:13; Romans 9:1; Ephesians 4:15

14

Pay Attention

Pay attention and listen to the sayings of the wise;
apply your heart to what I teach.
Proverbs 22:17

Pay attention to the wise people around you. It may be a child, a co-worker, a corporate executive, a custodian, a critic or a caregiver. The Lord places people in our lives who are full of truth and insight, but we have to be looking and listening to benefit. You may not like their tone of voice, but don't lose the truth of their words. Wisdom is waiting for an entrance into your ears, so listen expectantly and invite it into your understanding.

Pay attention to the current circumstances surrounding you. What is the Almighty saying in the middle of adversity and trials? Is His will to give up or to go on? How can you be creative since past strategies have lost their momentum? If something is not working, wisdom says to try something else. Attention to raw reality is enough reason to evaluate and become better. Perhaps you enroll in graduate school, or sell a high maintenance asset. It's during downturns that we are more determined to be the most effective.

Pay attention to your limitations, focus on less and learn to accept nothing less than excellence. As you grow older and your energy level decreases, your wisdom level should increase. Thus, it's imperative that wisdom moves from your head to your heart. Truth is the most freeing when it is transformative. The transition of truth from your head to your heart brings change. How is Christ changing you? Have you learned to become better?

Lastly, pay attention to the opportunities around you. Opportunities to serve, give, pray, encourage, rebuke, listen, learn, love, steward, invest, spend and save. Normally you find what you are looking for and you receive what you expect. Therefore, pray for the Holy Spirit to make you keenly aware of His leadership and work. Pay attention to the still small voice of Providence and obey, "And after the earthquake a fire; but the LORD was not in the fire: and after the fire a still small voice" (1 Kings 19:12, KJV).

In what environments do I best hear the voice and wisdom of God? How often will I go there?

Related Readings: Psalm 49:3; Proverbs 2:2-5; Isaiah 55:3; Matthew 17:5

Leaders of Integrity

But select capable men from all the people—men who fear God, trustworthy men who hate dishonest gain—and appoint them as officials over thousands, hundreds, fifties and tens.
Exodus 18:21

Leaders with integrity are a rare breed within a group of citizens whose utmost concern is, "What is in it for me?" A selfish society does not always select a leader for their integrity, but for their ability to manipulate a quick fix for chronic problems. It is this short sightedness that can set back a generation because of their leader's greed and corruption.

However, men and women of integrity understand the big picture of principled leadership, and they value fear of God, trustworthiness and honest economics. A leader of integrity looks out over the long term, and discovers what is best for the culture, its citizens, churches and families. There is a resolve to do the right things, with the right people, for the right reasons. Leaders of integrity integrate uprightness with their quiet influence.

"Then the LORD said to Satan, 'Have you considered my servant Job? There is no one on earth like him; he is blameless and upright, a man who fears God and shuns evil. And he still maintains his integrity, though you incited me against him to ruin him without any reason'" (Job 2:3).

Therefore, select capable men and women who hold Christ and His commands in high esteem, whom you can trust to do and say the right things, implemented in the right way. Leaders of integrity surround themselves with leaders of integrity. There is a high standard in their selection of leaders, because they want to represent the people extremely well. Competence and character are valued over loyal but incompetent friends with suspicious standards of behavior. A leader of integrity delegates to capable leaders.

So, select your leaders in government and church prayerfully, and only after extensive due diligence of their policies, integrity and track record. Blindly betting on one person is a bad process. Instead, select statesmen who will serve the people in the best interests of the country—who surround themselves with the best and the brightest, full of character. Most importantly, choose those who will submit to the accountability of God and man.

The early church experienced a similar selection process of leaders: "Brothers, choose seven men from among you who are known to be full of the Spirit and wisdom. We will turn this responsibility over to them and will give our attention to prayer and the ministry of the word" (Acts 6:3-4).

Who will I select as a leader that is best for my country, my family and my God?

Related Readings: 1 Kings 9:3-5; Psalm 25:21; 78:72; Mark 12:14; 2 Corinthians 1:12

16

Walking Wisely

Thus you will walk in the ways of good men,
and keep to the paths of the righteous.
Proverbs 2:20

Walking wisely means you keep company with those who love and obey Christ. They are your influencers, because their values reflect the route you want to take in life. There is an alignment of purpose with people who pray together on behalf of the greater good of God's Kingdom. So walk with the crowd who is all about character building, service to others, growth, love for the Lord and obedience to His commands.

At work prayerfully partner with those who are principled in their business philosophy. Someone may have less skill and experience, but you can trust their heart to do what they say they will do. Moreover, do not negotiate with mediocre living, as it is distasteful in the mouth of your Master Jesus. Instead walk with those who raise you to righteous living.

"Walk with the wise and become wise, for a companion of fools suffers harm" (Proverbs 13:20).

Of course you are to reach out and care for sinners, but with the purpose of loving them to the Lord. God has placed you in the life of unbelievers to influence them toward heaven. Perhaps one day they will thank you for your patience and prayers. Walking wisely means you learn to do well by being with those who aspire intimacy with the Almighty. You walk with the ones who obey the One.

Furthermore, your family may need you to slow down, because you have run so far ahead they are unable to keep up and benefit from your presence. Walk with your sons and daughters while you can. Your leadership at work will advance in significance when your entire team walks with you in focus. Above all else, walk with the Lord and He will give you wisdom and insight into who to walk with and where.

"This is what the LORD says: 'Stand at the crossroads and look; ask for the ancient paths, ask where the good way is, and walk in it, and you will find rest for your souls.' But you said, 'We will not walk in it'" (Jeremiah 6:16).

Who do I need to cease walking with, who do I need to continue walking with, and who do I need to begin walking with?

Related Readings: Psalm 119:63-115; I Corinthians 5:11; Hebrews 6:12

17

A Sustainable Lifestyle

Surely God is my help; the Lord is the one who sustains me.
Psalm 54:4

A lifestyle is sustainable when the Lord is the sustainer. Behind every sustainable life is dependence on a Savior: to help in time of need—to provide calm in a crisis—to give perspective when feeling pressure and to slow down someone who is way too busy. The grace of God gives sustainability to a life paced by prayer and energized by faith in Jesus.

Are you involved in so many good initiatives, only to find yourself unable to keep up with your commitments? Is your pace of life without margin—unable to really invest in those who need you the most? Indeed, it is extremely important to take periodic audits of our pace of life and make sure we make room for real relational investments. A life is unsustainable, if it is always darting from one good deed to the next with no down time.

"Sustain me, my God, according to your promise, and I will live; do not let my hopes be dashed" (Psalm 119:116).

Sometimes it takes a restoration of joy in following Jesus to realign our hearts in rest with Him. Joyless living is drudgery and only contributes to fatigue and exhaustion. However, the Lord upholds His own—by His presence and the wisdom of His word. He is ever present to energize a seeking soul with His solace of strength, peace and perseverance.

Like a wilderness hiker without a backpack of supplies and no compass—is a life that wanders around without the sustenance of Scripture and the leadership of the Holy Spirit. A sustainable life has Almighty God as its architect and belief in Jesus as its builder. He sustains those who regularly seek Him with a pure heart and a teachable mind. He helps the humble and lifts up those who worship Him in Spirit and in truth.

"The LORD sustains the humble but casts the wicked to the ground" (Psalm 147:6).

Are you old? The Lord is your sustainer in your later years. Are you sick? Your Savior Jesus sustains you on your sick bed. Are you an orphan? You are not an outcast, but a precious child of your Heavenly Father. Are you a widow or widower? You are not alone, but loved by the Lord. Are you in a new country, away from home? Jesus is trustworthy in your transition. Are you afraid? Christ is a prayer away to provide comfort and care.

Lastly, a sustainable lifestyle happens in community with other followers of Jesus. Faith comes alive when it is exercised in the presence of other people who love the Lord. You feel support, love, compassion, prayers and wisdom from the Body of Christ. The Lord is your help and His people are His helpers. A sustainable lifestyle comes from Christ.

"The Son is the radiance of God's glory and the exact representation of his being, sustaining all things by his powerful word" (Hebrews 1:3a).

How can I sustain my lifestyle in the power of the Spirit and not in my own strength?

Related Readings: Job 36:19; Psalm 119:175; 146:9; Isaiah 46:4; 50:4; 59:16

18

Active Accountability

> But if you do warn the righteous man not to sin and he does
> not sin, he will surely live because he took warning,
> and you will have saved yourself.
> Ezekiel 3:21

Effective accountability partners are not passive. Once someone invites a friend into his or her life for accountability, it is a serious responsibility. Accountability is active, engaging, and encouraging. The giver and the receiver of accountability have entered into a trusting relationship. Indeed, wisdom listens to the warning of its accountability partner or group.

Authentic accountability requires caring confrontation. A little bit of short-term discomfort and embarrassment will save you a lot of long-term regret. Thus, when you encounter emotional situations, keep a level head. Accountability facilitates objectivity. When you are under pressure, you have an objective team that gives you wise perspective. Your accountability group is there as a buffer to unwise decision making.

"Better a poor but wise youth than an old but foolish king who no longer knows how to heed a warning" (Ecclesiastes 4:13).

Accountability provides much needed courage for another to do the right thing. Sometimes it is hard decisions that paralyze us into non-action. However, avoiding a difficult decision today will compound its inevitable consequences in the future. Accountability encourages you not to procrastinate when you are afraid. It relieves your fears and bolsters your faith.

For example, team members may need to be terminated for the good of the company and for their individual betterment. Prospective church volunteers may need to be told "no" because their character is not fitting for a leadership role. Your young adult children are not prepared for marriage because they need to first move out from home and experience independent living. Accountability helps everyone move forward in God's will.

Above all else, live like you are accountable to almighty God, as one day we all give an account to Him for our actions. "They are surprised that you do not join them in their reckless, wild living, and they heap abuse on you. But they will have to give account to Him who is ready to judge the living and the dead" (1 Peter 4:4–5).

Prayer: Am I truly accountable to others, and do I provide effective accountability to friends?

Related Readings: Proverbs 7:1–27; Jonah 3:6; Luke 17:1–4; Hebrews 4:13

Pursue Righteousness and Love

He who pursues righteousness and love finds life,
prosperity and honor.
Proverbs 21:21

Leaders who pursue righteousness and love are able to outlast calamity and criticism. They become principled men and women whose influence is attractive and valuable. People long for leaders who have their best interests and the best interests of the enterprise in mind. When you follow after righteousness, your followers follow after righteousness. Your right actions lead others to find life, prosperity and honor.

There is no genuine understanding of life without a relationship with the Lord. Your goal as a Christian leader is to get people to God. When people discover God's game plan, they understand "All the world is a stage, and all men and women are mere players". It is freeing to find their part in His story. Be who the Lord made you to be, and do not bow to being anyone else. Leaders lead people to find their identity in Christ, and thus trust Him.

Leaders who lead out of love, lead others to love. Righteousness is reciprocal. When an organization is set on loving others into success, they will be successful. Secure leaders can see the hidden potential in people who lack confidence, and through patient prayer and instruction, lead them to be productive team members. "So then we pursue the things which make for peace and the building up of one another" (Romans 14:19, NASB).

Lastly, when the waters of righteousness and love rise in a ministry, business, or home, the boats of life, prosperity and honor, rise as well. Your standard of accepted behavior at work may be, "You don't have to believe in Jesus, but you do have to behave like Jesus." The Lord rewards wise pursuits: "The reward of humility and the fear of the LORD are riches, honor and life" (Proverbs 22:4, NASB).

Are my pursuits pleasing to my heavenly Father? Am I a leader worth following? Do I follow the servant leadership of my Savior?

Related Readings: Isaiah 51:1; Hosea 6:3; Romans 2:7-10; Hebrews 12:14

Strengths and Struggles

We have different gifts, according to the grace given us.
Romans 12:6a

Know and understand your strengths, for it's best to behave how God created you. By God's grace, He places within you giftedness to carry out His plan. This is called your core competency. You may be a gifted leader, so lead. You may be a gifted coach, so coach. You may be a gifted counselor, so counsel. You may be a gifted administrator, so administer.

You may be a gifted networker, so network. You may be a gifted writer, so write. You may be a gifted teacher, so teach. You may be a gifted servant, so serve. You may be a gifted artist, so create. You may be a gifted communicator, so communicate. There is a long menu of gifts, and you probably resemble several of them. Study your gifts, and you will discover your strengths.

Become comfortable with and accept the one thing you do naturally. It is effortless because God has engineered you for this. He gave you the skills and abilities to innovate, create, and produce these desired outcomes. However, make sure you do not confuse passion with strength. If you have the passion to speak, it is imperative you at least have the raw skill for speaking. Many of the technicalities of communication can be learned, but don't try to make yourself become someone you're not.

Synergy for life and work come as you align passions and strengths. Take the time to understand what you do best and where you have the most energy, and then position your responsibilities at home and work to mirror that ideal. Do not be afraid to change and try new things. Ask others to validate what you do best. Ask those who know you well to affirm where they see your passion protrude. Then, prayerfully align around both.

You can know and understand your strengths by taking a spiritual gifts test as this helps you define your God given disposition. Take a personality assessment, for this helps you understand your temperament. Lastly, consider taking a psychological test, because this reveals your emotional intelligence and your leadership style. Be who God has made you to be and you will be free.

Furthermore, embrace and celebrate your struggles. They keep you humble. Do not resist accepting your struggles; embrace them instead. Make your struggles your servant by allowing others to do much better what you can't do. It is okay not to like details, but value them and those who manage them well. Your struggles beg the need for a team. It is in your struggles that you depend more on God and others.

So, be honest with yourself about what you don't do well. Accept the fact that even though you want to do something, you don't need to if others can do it better. They can free you to do what only you can do. Release your areas of mediocre effectiveness, as this gives others opportunities for excellence. Laugh at yourself, for this frees you from the tension of unrealistic expectations, and allows you to enjoy life.

You are a valued member in the Body of Christ. "The body is a unit, though it is made up of many parts; and though all its parts are many, they form one body. So it is with Christ. For we were all baptized by one Spirit into one body…" (1 Corinthians 12:12-13a).

Prayer: Dear Lord thank you for the good times and the tough times and for growing me into the likeness of your son Jesus.

Related Readings: 1 Corinthians 12:4-6; Philippians 4:13; 2 Kings 22:19

Focus On Today

Therefore do not worry about tomorrow, for tomorrow will worry
about itself. Each day has enough trouble of its own.
Matthew 6:34

Focus on today, for it is the only day you can directly influence with your actions. Today is the best day to do what you have put off doing. Your motivation of love casts out fear. So go ahead and confront your circumstances with confidence knowing Christ is leading you. Use today to trust the Lord with your relationships and the results of your work.

Why do we worry instead of taking responsibility? One reason is worry gives us an excuse to do nothing and then expect someone else to be responsible for our irresponsible behavior. But this is not the path of a mature Christian who really believes God is in control. Believers steeped in Scripture know they have to do their part and trust the Lord with His part. Worry precludes responsibility, while prayerful trust seizes the day.

Do you feel overwhelmed in your new role? Does it seem like you work and worry more than ever? Is your leadership at a point of breaking under the weight of everyone else's expectations? It is in times of intense pressure that we lean into the Lord. Prayer is the pressure valve to release your anxieties. Ask, what does God want me to do today?

Today brings enough of its own burdens and grievances, yet it is complimented by daily doses of grace and strength to sustain you. Grace under fire is your test to show friends and foes a gracious response. Prepare for tomorrow, but do not obsess over its uncertainty. Focus on today – then your faith will flourish and your work will prosper.

Therefore, in your quiet place before the Lord, inhale His peace and exhale your anxiety. Look around you at the faithfulness of God in the lives of those who endure with a smile. Your calm assurance is a refuge of hope for friends, family and co-workers who suffer in silence. Today, stay the course of your trust in Christ for you facilitate faith for others.

"So, as the Holy Spirit says: 'Today, if you hear his voice, do not harden your hearts as you did in the rebellion, during the time of testing in the desert'" (Hebrews 3:7-8).

What can I do today to trust God with tomorrow? Who can I encourage to not worry, but to hope for the Lord's provision?

Related Readings: Deuteronomy 5:24; Psalm 95:6-8; Proverbs 22:19; Hebrews 11:39-40

22

Character Is Resourceful

In her hand she holds the distaff and grasps
the spindle with her fingers.
Proverbs 31:19

Sometimes you can make things cheaper and better than you can buy them. This is being resourceful. Do you find yourself trying to make ends meet and just paying the bills? Maybe there are some creative alternatives to cash. Consider bartering with a friend. You can babysit for each other and save the expense of paying someone to watch your child.

In the past at work you have been accustomed to a fat budget for generating new business, but now your resources are lean or non-existent. Is there another professional relationship you could trade for your expertise? Perhaps your ability to coach someone in executive leadership could be exchanged for their access to web development. It is during tight times that creativity and resourcefulness reign. Think outside the box and it will grow.

The early church understood how to be resourceful in taking care of one another. "And all the believers lived in a wonderful harmony, holding everything in common. They sold whatever they owned and pooled their resources so that each person's need was met" (Acts 2:43 TM). Is there something you need to sell so that someone else's needs could be met?

Consider innovative alternatives to current issues and you will be freed from the status quo. Resourcefulness often requires patience because it takes more time to research and connect the proper relationships, but it is fulfilling knowing you stewarded the Lord's resources by faith and with frugality. Ask God for wisdom in how to creatively come up with unconventional solutions. He will lead you in ways you may not have even considered.

Cling to Christ, the ultimate Creator. "I form the light and create darkness, I bring prosperity and create disaster; I, the LORD, do all these things" (Isaiah 45:7).

Jesus is radically resourceful. When I run out of ideas do I run to Him for help and think creatively? What are some resourceful ways I can prayerfully meet our pressing needs?

Related Readings: Psalm 111:5; Ezekiel 18:7; Matthew 21:2; Luke 9:13-15

Perseverance's Prize

The temple was finished in all its details according to its specifications. He had spent seven years building it. It took Solomon thirteen years, however, to complete the construction of his palace.
1 Kings 6:38 b, 7:1

Sometimes it is difficult to finish. Just the sound of the word perseverance communicates something difficult. But do not quit–press on–it would be easy to quit now, but later you will be glad you finished. Perseverance is required because most projects, people and life goals require more than we anticipated. Yes, our expectations normally "under bid" the cost of the commitment. We get in the middle of our commitment and realize the need for more patience, forgiveness and determination than we originally budgeted.

The extra cost of time and money can be discouraging and even depressing. The business or ministry you started with great enthusiasm is now struggling. It requires much more time, leadership and money than you would have ever dreamed. The children you are raising are a joy, but at times can be painful and require great grace. Your marriage is mostly heaven, but at times can be like hell, so stay loyal to your vows. How do you respond when the going gets rough? Life is not fair, so how will you persevere? We persevere because the results are rewarding. The process conforms us into the likeness of Christ. His character becomes a rock of dependability during hard times. So how do we persevere during adversity?

First, you are able to persevere by going to Jesus. Every other place you can turn will be lacking. Ultimately it is your Heavenly Father who has the answers. He is the dependable one who never leaves us or forsakes us. Jesus understands perseverance as He "endured the cross and despised its shame" (Hebrews 12:2, KJV). He didn't give up–for our sake.

Another reason we are able to persevere is the past and present example of others. People throughout history have paid the ultimate price so that we might enjoy our freedoms. Closer to home you have family members who have toiled relentlessly so you could enjoy the fruits of their labors. How can we give up, when those before us, in more difficult circumstances, were able to persevere? Gratitude produces perseverance.

Lastly, there is a good pride that says, "I will complete this goal because it is the right thing to do. I have made this commitment, thus I will finish". Once you have completed the task, you can relish the moment for years to come, knowing you never gave up, you gave it your best and you persevered. Persevere for Christ's sake and the sake of others; you will be so satisfied with the results. Your perseverance gives others hope to press on.

"You have persevered and have endured hardships for my name, and have not grown weary" (Revelations 2:3).

What project or job do I need to see through to completion? Will I persevere for Him?

Related Readings: Romans 5:3-4; 1 Corinthians 13:7; Hebrews 11:27; 2 Thessalonians 3:5

Vocational Fulfillment

When his master saw that the LORD was with him and that the LORD gave him success in everything he did, Joseph found favor in his eyes and became his attendant. Potiphar put him in charge of his household, and he entrusted to his care everything he owned.
Genesis 39:3-4

What brings you fulfillment in your work? Is it the sense of accomplishment? Is it the opportunity to encourage someone? Is it the satisfaction of caring for your family? Is it the sense of security from a steady income stream? Your vocational fulfillment flows from a combination of these characteristics and more. When you are fulfilled in your job you are able to filter through the negatives on the way to the positives.

Be careful not to equate feeling passionate about your position with being fulfilled in your work. Passions ebb and flow around the excitement of a situation, like a start-up when everyone is thinking and working 24/7. But this break neck passionate pace is not sustainable. Your career is a marathon not a sprint. Indeed, if you are absorbed in your work and not constantly glancing at the clock, then perhaps you are in a place of fulfillment.

Is it your sense of control over the outcome that draws you to serve where you work? You feel empowered, you are able to expand your skills and you can make a meaningful contribution in your community as a parent or an employee. Vocational fulfillment flows from a heart engaged in a mission that means something to you and to the Lord.

If Christ has placed you where you are, can you be content to serve Him wholeheartedly? The Almighty's vocational assignment carries its own sense of satisfaction. Joseph found favor because God placed him in his leadership role. In the same way use your workplace platform as a launching pad for the Lord. Your ability to support others, offer promotions and create a caring culture facilitates fulfillment for everyone.

Vocational fulfillment is a faith journey that brings out the best in you and those around you. God blesses the work He assigns. Have you accepted the Lord's assignment? "From the time he put him in charge of his household and of all that he owned, the LORD blessed the household of the Egyptian because of Joseph" (Genesis 39:5a).

What brings me fulfillment in my job? How can I help others find fulfillment in their work?

Related Readings: Genesis 6:22; Exodus 35:30-32; 1 Corinthians 12:28; 1 Peter 4:10-11

25

Stand Your Ground

The wicked man flees though no one pursues,
but the righteous are as bold as a lion.
Proverbs 28:1

Boldness comes from being with Christ. He empowers the righteous to do the right things the right way. It is out of your intimacy with the Almighty that you are empowered to engage the enemy and endure hardships. Indeed, the fruit of great challenges is great rewards. So stand your ground for God and do not give in to fear and doubt. If you rely on yourself you will fail, but if you rely on the Lord you will succeed.

Self-reliance crumbles when circumstances become grim. People without God as their guide run away in fear, but the righteous take heart and hold on to heaven's inheritance. They are bold and remain strong because they see their Savior Jesus as the initiator and completer of the cause. However, as you remain poised in prayer to God, take the time to grow your leadership and give to others the resources they need to succeed.

Followers need a leader who is not caught up in self-preservation, but captivated by Christ. A bold leader is not preoccupied with an exit strategy. Rather, he or she is focused on how to process problems with creative solutions. A culture of confidence takes root when everyone is committed to thriving in excellence, not just surviving in mediocrity. Fear sees failure behind every challenge, but faith sees opportunity rise out of anguish.

Therefore, stand your ground with God. The enemy has no authority over you, especially your emotions. His is a phantom pursuit. Stay rooted in righteous acts with a hopeful attitude and Almighty God will bless your efforts. You are bold when you have been with Jesus. "When they saw the courage of Peter and John and realized that they were unschooled, ordinary men, they were astonished and they took note that these men had been with Jesus" (Acts 4:13).

Is my security in myself or in my Savior Jesus Christ?

Related Readings: 2 Kings 7:6-7; Psalm 53:5; Acts 14:3; 1 Thessalonians 2:2

26

A Good Name

A good name is more desirable than great riches;
to be esteemed is better than silver and gold.
Proverbs 22:1

Are you willing to sacrifice your good name for the gain of great riches? Is it worth diluting your influence and soiling your reputation? What price can you put on your good name? It is your most valuable asset, because it says you are not willing to sell out at any price. A noble name is a like a rare gold coin from antiquity: priceless and desirable. Like David, apply appropriate actions. "David behaved himself more wisely than all the servants of Saul. So his name was highly esteemed" (1 Samuel 18:30b, NASB).

What is a good name? It is given by God; for God. A good name makes sure to give God the glory for its good deeds. Its fortress is the fear of the Lord, which keeps out unwanted influences. A good name follows through with what it says. It is neither passive aggressive or aggressive passive for it is forthright in both speech and motives. A good name means you stand for something good, and you are willing to suffer loss for what's right. You believe God blesses obedience, not manipulation for money's sake.

How do you keep your good name intact? Humility and honor are twin pillars that support the edifice of a respectable reputation. No matter what degree of success you experience you are quick to share the limelight with the Lord and those who contributed to your good fortune. When we grasp for the credit we discredit our leadership. It is in giving that we get to grow our good name. Humility is the hinge on which honor turns.

Lastly, honor God and man, and your name will be honored. Respect is reciprocal. For example, you honor a contract, even when circumstances have changed for the negative. You are willing to lose a new lease because you promised your tenant a 30-day notice. The Lord blesses landlords that keep their word and who long to do the right thing. Indeed, your honor and good name depend on God, "My salvation and my honor depend on God; he is my mighty rock, my refuge" (Psalm 62:7).

Thus, is my goal to grow my good name, or to gain wealth? Do I honor God and people in the process? How valuable is my good name?

Related Readings: 1 Kings 1:47; Ecclesiastes 7:1; Luke 2:52; Acts 10:22

27

Leaders Are Learners

What do you know that we do not know?
What insights do you have that we do not have?
Job 15:9

Leaders who stay enrolled in God's school of learning are wiser. You have learned tremendous lessons over the years, but this is just the beginning. Stay in the educational process. We never arrive as learners. Teachability should only cease after our graduation into heaven. Indeed, great leaders want to follow leaders who are learners.

Effective leaders know that a growing leader will pass on his or her learning experiences. Great leaders grow leaders! And there is a good chance what you are currently learning as a leader is the same lesson someone else is struggling to conquer. Your ability to stay engaged in the learning process allows you to tutor other leaders facing the same issues.

When we stop learning we cease to be relevant, we become stale and our influence begins to wane. Learning keeps us engaged with our team and with other leaders. Moreover, a wise leader understands the learning curve required to tackle new issues and problems. Every day there are opportunities that beg for attention and understanding. This means greater wisdom is required. Gratefully, the Lord gives wisdom liberally to those who ask:

"If any of you lacks wisdom, he should ask God, who gives generously to all without finding fault, and it will be given to him" (James 1:5).

Furthermore, learn from everyone and everything around you. Educated and uneducated, rich and poor, young and old are all teacher candidates. God places people in our lives daily as His teachers. Perhaps you study the life of people from the past. You can read biographies, book reviews and historical novels. Deceased people are rich with life lessons to be harvested and stored in your barn of knowledge, both positive and negative examples.

Learn how they sacrificed their family to gain business success, then avoid the same mistakes. Discover how successful leaders from the past influenced men and women for a greater good and follow their example. Dissect the lives of great leaders placing the pieces of their lives under the microscope of God's word and the scrutiny of your experience. Then you can extract truth and discover patterns of success.

Of course feasting on the classics is imperative to the leader who is hungry to learn. Read books together and discuss them as a leadership team. Expose yourself to their timeliness and you will find yourself lost in learning. Your mind and heart will travel to uncharted waters and places where others have not feared to fail and succeed.

The classics will challenge you to become a critical thinker and to look beyond the surface for great nuggets of truth. Why mess around with the milk of easy thinking when we can plunge into the meat of issues great thinkers have wrestled with over centuries? Most importantly, feed on the wisdom of God's word. Holy Scripture is your number one source for truth. Wise leaders apply the practical principles for living found in the Bible.

"Do your best to present yourself to God as one approved, a workman who does not need to be ashamed and who correctly handles the word of truth" (2 Timothy 2:15).

What is God teaching me as a leader? Am I embracing and applying His wisdom?

Related Readings: Exodus 18:24-26; I Kings 4:29; John 12:42; Romans 12:8

28

Integrity Lost

Her leaders judge for a bribe, her priests teach for a price,
and her prophets tell fortunes for money.
Micah 3:11

Integrity is not for sale to those who love their Savior, Jesus. There is no amount of money or status that can lure integrity away from someone who values its influence, accountability, and positive outcomes. Integrity is your calling card for leadership and it is evidence of your faith in Christ.

Integrity may be your greatest value that is not itemized on your balance sheet, and is not for sale with serious followers of the Lord. Like Esau selling his birthright (Genesis 25:25-34), you can let your appetites lead you to exchange your integrity for instant gratification, but it's a lopsided loss to let go of a lifetime of faithfulness for a moment of problematic pleasure.

Moreover, the love of money makes you vulnerable to losing your integrity (1 Timothy 6:10). Money can maneuver your motives into a less than desirable position, so be sure not to masquerade your good works around a drive for wealth. You cannot reason your way around wrong methods of obtaining money, even for the sake of worthy outcomes. You do not have to compromise your God-given convictions to grow your net worth.

Effective leaders, in the long run, are given respect, trust, and goodwill because of their position, authority, and track record of integrity. How much is your credibility worth? Certainly it is more valuable than anything money can buy (Proverbs 22:1). Indeed, integrity is being true to yourself and to God's calling on your life, so be who you are in Him. Integrity does not have to prove itself. Rather, it rests in being itself. Align your doing around your being, for this integration is the essence of integrity.

Furthermore, if you have lost your integrity, it can be found in Christ. So, go to Him in honesty and humility. Be forthright with your heavenly Father about your failures and blown opportunities. Let Him love you through this time of transition and rebuilding of trust. It will take time for those who have been hurt to begin healing and reconciliation. But the longer you prove to yourself and others that you are the real deal, the more your integrity will blossom. A track record of faithfulness fertilizes the roots of integrity and produces lasting fruit. Cultivate integrity through prayer and service, then watch it grow.

Take the time to do what you say you will do, because follow through and consistency create credibility. Invest in others so they don't feel you have used them merely to accomplish your agenda. Integrity insists on doing what's right, in the right way, and at the right time. Integrity does not belittle others or get caught up in the seduction of stuff.

Integrity gains traction through gratitude for God's grace, instead of losing its footing on money's ledge of allegiance. Integrity provides peace and stability, and is found by walking with your Lord. "The man of integrity walks securely, but he who takes crooked paths will be found out" (Proverbs 10:9). Therefore, gain it, retain it, and do not sell it out at any price.

Prayer: Heavenly Father by Your grace keep my motives upright before You.

Related Readings: 1 Chronicles 29:17; Nehemiah 7:2; Job 2:3; Job 27:5-6; Psalm 25:21; Psalm 41:12

29

Follow Up

Moses inspected the work and saw that they had done it just
as the LORD had commanded. So Moses blessed them.
Exodus 39:43

Follow-up is necessary for effective leadership. It is necessary in your work and family. It is necessary as you manage and hold others responsible. Follow-up means you care about the person who is performing the task and you care about the work being done. You follow up with your children because you care for them too much not to stay involved in their lives. They may seem distant and disinterested, but you still follow up.

Relationships retreat for lack of follow-up. Ego and pride resist follow-up and then we expect others to initiate, but people forget. People do not place as high a priority on your activities as you do. They may even commit to a certain time, but because of busyness, fail to follow through. Extremely active people need more follow-up than is normally necessary. You may feel rejected when a person appears disinterested. They may be, but you are responsible to provide gentle reminders and reengage them at a more robust level. Effective follow-up is as much an art as a science. Have a systematic style to your communications, but do not badger people by bombarding them with too much, too often.

People do better when you "inspect what we expect." So, take the time to inspect. Create margin for inspection and accountability. Follow-up is an appropriate time to revisit expectations. The longer disconnected expectations are left unaddressed, the higher the probability for misunderstanding and failure. Frequent inspection leads to clarification and correction. Small adjustments along the way defuse frustrations and avert subtle surprises down the road.

Do not assume that someone understands the first time. Don't assume you understand the first time. Make sure everyone is on the same page and that there is a coalition of efforts and resources. Also, be willing to adjust, as thinking and engaged people will discover a better way of doing things. Encourage and reward their wise and resourceful innovation. Follow-up frees people to give much needed feedback.

Above all else, make sure the project and the process revolve around God's principles of work and relationships. It is imperative that everyone be aligned around the Almighty's agenda. His way is the best way; so do not compromise the non-negotiables that define the values and mission of the enterprise.

Follow-up keeps a focus on the purpose of glorifying God. Follow-up is for the purpose of wise stewardship, excellent communication, and affirming accountability. Use your frequent follow-up as a way to bless the other person. Make the follow-up of the transaction or task a small percentage of the conversation.

Use this excuse for relational engagement to find out about the person. Listen for their fears, their frustrations, and their dreams. People want to know they are cared for before they care to listen. Follow-up leads to follow through, all for a greater purpose than any one individual.

Use your faithful follow-up as an opportunity to bless others on behalf of God. For example, Paul wrote out expectations and then followed up in person. "Although I hope to come to you soon, I am writing you these instructions so that, if I am delayed, you will know how people ought to conduct themselves in God's household, which is the church of the living God, the pillar and foundation of the truth" (1 Timothy 3:14-15).

Prayer: Heavenly Father give me the focus and energy to follow up for Your glory.

Related Readings: 1 Kings 6:12-13; Exodus 39:42-43; Leviticus 14:39-42; Hebrews 10:24-25

30

Right Results, Wrong Methods

"The Lord said to Moses...speak to that rock.... Moses said to them, 'Listen you rebels, must we bring you water out of this rock?' Then Moses raised his arm and struck the rock twice with his staff. Water gushed out.... But the Lord said to Moses and Aaron, 'Because you did not trust in me to honor me as holy in the sight of the Israelites, you will not bring this community into the land I give them.'"
Numbers 20:7-8a, 10b, 12

Right results are not the measurement of success. How you arrive at the results is even more important. It is not all about results, though they are important, done the right way. Pragmatism is not king. Christ is King. Christ cares as much or more about our methods as He does about our results. He may even bless our bad attitude in the short term, but He still requires our confession and repentance.

A bad attitude leads to wrong methods. There is no getting around this. You cannot lower yourself to lash back at the ingratitude and immaturity of others. Cool off and pray before you angrily give them what they want. If you cave in to coercion, then you are a good candidate for doing the right thing the wrong way. Then you may remorsefully get the right results and bypass the use of wise methods.

This can happen as easily at home as at work. Do not blow up at your children and give them their way just because they whine and complain. This is a recipe for rebellion in their teenage years. Early on they learn how to manipulate your emotions. Indeed, an environment of fatigue and frustration is not conducive to wise decision making, and certainly not the best time to execute your decisions. Anger is like a large, dull knife. It gets results but the process is jagged and bloody.

Before you launch off into a direction of leadership, make sure that you have a defined process of wise methods and accurate measurements. Create these out of a calm and cool head. Do not act in a way that you later will regret. Previously planned processes are in place for your protection. These are checks and balances to assure excellence in execution.

God is very interested in our methods. He expects to be honored and respected in the process of getting results. Running over people to reach your goal is an inaccurate reflection of the Lord you serve. However, if you serve people in the process of reaching the agreed upon goal, you illustrate the heart of Jesus.

So much hinges on our spirit, attitude and actions. This is a trilogy that reflects right methods. Yes, methods need to be modified for efficiency and effectiveness, but this can be done through dialogue, not dictating. People are respected when the rationale is explained around a change in procedures. The best ideas can come from those responsible to implement them. Listen keenly to the voice of reason.

Wisdom resides here. You do not have to rush to get results out of fear of failure. You can wait, pray and define a planned process that is derived from collaboration with the team. Then your work is sustainable and everyone is honored in the process. Focus on the right methods, and the right results will take care of themselves. Always remind yourself of how Christ would behave. It is the spirit of Jesus that cultivates the right attitudes and actions. Trust and honor God with the process and in the process. Then, the right methods will support the right results!

Prayer: Dear Lord help me do Your work, Your way for Your glory.

Related Readings: Proverbs 11:1; Genesis 30:33; 2 Kings 12:13-16; Isaiah 59:14

WHAT READERS ARE SAYING ABOUT WISDOM HUNTERS

I LOVE this devotional "New Normal". I went through a divorce after 20 years of marriage. It's been three years and my 2 kids and I have moved 3 times, both kids changed schools, I changed jobs twice. I have NEVER had this much upheaval in my entire life. But… God is faithful. We are learning to live differently. We are learning to trust God irrationally. We are learning to lean on Him as the father/husband of our family. We are learning who God is in such a real way. Thanks for the encouragement! – Pam

Thank you for these scripture inspirations. I have them on my mirror to memorize and meditate on during this hectic, busy time of year. Focus on Him in all we do. – Mary

The Wisdom Hunters Devotionals are so helpful thank you for them and the Christmas Scripture Cards. Their value is inconceivable. Thank You again! May the Lord Bless You and Your Family. Merry Christmas – Don

Boyd, my refrigerator is not large enough for all the golden nuggets in this message!! Especially helpful to me was, "…God's desire is to come alongside you and realign your cares with what He cares about the most……God's system of care is countercultural……Equally spiritual people may cast their cares on God in polar opposite ways……allow Him to do what He does best…..This takes humility on your part……..What started out as a burden, He transforms into a blessing. Your pain becomes productive……..An all-caring God cultivates a carefree attitude………Let God be consumed with your cares so you are not…….You can care because you have let Him care for you.Keep the circle of care rotating…….Thank you very much!! – Diane

This may be my favorite one so far. God used this to speak to me that just because we fear doesn't mean He's forgotten us. Also, He uses EVRYTHING for our good. I like how you made it personal. We need that, to see that our brothers and sisters are being real and vulnerable. Thank you. – Jacqueline

Thank you for this message of truth. A grateful follower of your online ministry. – Vivian

Wow! This message was right to the point. I asked God to reveal something that was weighing heavy on my heart, and He not only did He surfaced it the light but but granted the truth to me that I hsve been discerning in my spirits. Also to forgive myself for holding back all the hurt and forgiveness and the things I did or how I too behaved like a puppet on a string to please others. Thank you once again for a powerful insight and message along with the prayer of hope and scripters to read. God bless you and your ministry. May the Lord keep blessing you with His heavenly treasures to prosper over your lives. Love & Much Blessings Always. – Rhonda

Once again, this was exactly what I needed! It is such a blessing to have these words at my disposal each day. especially now. we are going through such harsh financial and health trials, but our faith is daily uplifted through your website. thank you and may God continue to bless you and your wonderful ministry. – Sondra

Thank you for what you do, the words you say, pray, and share. I have been out of work for over 4 years now and had a good solid lead on a job…today I found I was not selected….this news hurt, I felt rejected again, felt lost and wondered why God is not anwsering my prayers. I needed this message today, it spoke to my heart and made me weep. Thank you! - Becky

AMEN! I am asking God to purify my motives, and only do things for Him and His glory! Thank you this is an awesome and thought provoking devotion. God bless you! – Jenny

I do support your ministry and want you to know every time I read (most every day !) I am always blessed and encouraged to seek to know Him better and trust Him. A lot of times I print my email and give it to someone who God puts in my path and prompts me to give it to them. Thank you for sharing in such a bold and heartfelt manner! You are appreciated and a blessing to the body! – Cathy

- ECNWIÒG A DISCIPLE N6 JESUS CHRIST

Wy journey that led me to God covered a span of 19 years, before I truly understood my need for His love and forgiveness in a personal relationship with Jesus Christ. Along this path of spiritual awakening, God placed many people along the way as spiritual guideposts directing me toward Him.

Initially it was my mother who took me to church at age 12 so I could learn about faith through the confirmation process. Wy grandmother was a role model in her walk with Jesus by being kind and generous to all she encountered. Nnce in college, I began attending church with Rita (my future wife) and her family.

It was then that relevant weekly teaching from an ancient book—the - ible—began to answer many of life.s.questions. It intrigued me: 4 hat is God.s.plan for my life? 4 ho is Jesus Christ? 4 hat are sin, salvation, heaven and hell? How can I live an B abundant life of forgiveness, joy and love?

So, the Lord found me first with His incredible love and when I surrendered in repentance and faith in Jesus, I found Him. 6or two years a businessman in our church showed me how to grow in grace through - ible study, prayer, faith sharing and service to others. I still discover each day more of God.s.great love and His new mercies.

Below is an outline for finding God and becoming a disciple of Jesus:

1. BELIEVE: ! If you declare with your mouth, ! Jesus is Lord," and believe in your heart that God raised him from the dead, you will be saved" (Romans 10:9). - elief in Jesus Christ as your Savior and Lord gives you eternal life in heaven.

2. REPENT AND BE BAPTIZED: ! Peter replied, 'Repent and be baptized, every one of you, in the name of Jesus Christ for the forgiveness of your sins. And you will receive the gift of the Holy Spirit.". (Acts 2:3F). Repentance means you turn from your sin and publically confess Christ in baptism.

3. OBEY: ! Jesus replied, 'Anyone who loves me will obey my teaching. Wy 6ather will love them, and we will come to them and make our home with them.". (John 1M23). Nbedience is an indicator of our love for the Lord Jesus and His presence in our life.

4. WORSHIP, PRAYER, COMMUNITY, EVANGELISM AND STUDY: ! Every day they continued to meet together in the temple

courts. They broke bread in their homes and ate together with glad and sincere hearts, praising God and enjoying the favor of all the people. And the Lord added to their number daily those who were being saved" (Acts 2:MBM). 4 orship and prayer are our expressions of gratitude and honor to God and our dependence on His grace. Community and evangelism are our accountability to Christians and compassion for nonBChristians. Study to apply the knowledge, understanding, and wisdom of God.

5. LOVE GOD: ! Jesus replied: 'Love the Lord your God with all your heart and with all your soul and with all your mind…This is the first and greatest commandment" (Watthew 22:37BF). Intimacy with the almighty God is a growing and loving relationship. 4 e are loved by Him, so we can love others and be empowered by the Holy Spirit to obey His commands.

6. LOVE PEOPLE: ! And the second is like it: 'Love your neighbor as yourself.". (Watthew 22:39). Loving people is an outflow of the love for our heavenly 6ather. 4 e are able to love because He first loved us.

7. MAKE DISCIPLES: ! And the things you have heard me say in the presence of many witnesses entrust to reliable people who will also be qualified to teach others" (2 Timothy 2:2). The reason we disciple others is because we are extremely grateful to God and to those who disciple us, and we want to obey Christ.s.last instructions before going to heaven.

MEET THE AUTHOR

Boyd Bailey

Boyd Bailey, the author of Wisdom Hunters devotionals, is the founder of Wisdom Hunters, Inc., an Atlanta-based ministry created to encourage Christians (a.k.a wisdom hunters) to *apply God's unchanging Truth in a changing world.*

By God's grace, Boyd has impacted wisdom hunters in over 86 countries across the globe through the Wisdom Hunters daily devotion, wisdomhunters.com devotional blog and devotional books.

For over 30 years Boyd Bailey has passionately pursued wisdom through his career in fulltime ministry, executive coaching, and mentoring.

Since becoming a Christian at the age of 19, Boyd begins each day as a wisdom hunter, diligently searching for Truth in scripture, and through God's grace, applying it to his life.

These raw, 'real time' reflections from his personal time with the Lord, are now impacting over 111,000 people through the Wisdom Hunters Daily Devotion email. In addition to the daily devotion, Boyd has authored nine devotional books: *Infusion*, a 90-day devotional, *Seeking Daily the Heart of God Vol I & II*, 365-day devotionals *Seeking God in the Proverbs*, a 90-day devotional and *Seeking God in the Psalms*, a 90-day devotional along with several 30-day devotional e-Books on topics such as *Wisdom for Fathers, Wisdom for Mothers, Wisdom for Graduates,* and *Wisdom for Marriage.*

In addition to Wisdom Hunters, Boyd is the co-founder and CEO of Ministry Ventures, a faith based non-profit, where he has trained and coached over 1000 ministries in the best practices of prayer, board, ministry models, administration and fundraising. Prior to Ministry Ventures, Boyd was the National Director for Crown Financial Ministries and an Associate Pastor at First Baptist Church of Atlanta. Boyd serves on numerous boards including Ministry Ventures, Wisdom Hunters, Atlanta Mission, Souly Business and Blue Print for Life.

Boyd received his Bachelor of Arts from Jacksonville State University and his Masters of Divinity from Southwestern Seminary. He and Rita, his wife of 30 plus years, live in Roswell, Georgia and are blessed with four daughters, three sons-in-law who love Jesus, two granddaughters and two grandsons. Boyd and Rita enjoy missions and investing in young couples, as well as hiking, reading, traveling, working through their bucket list, watching college football, and hanging out with their kids and grandkids whenever possible.

27140445R00044

Made in the USA
Charleston, SC
02 March 2014